THE JANE HISSEY COLLECTION

OLD BEAR
ADDRESS BOOK

First published in 1991 by Ebury Press Stationery
An imprint of the Random Century Group
Random Century House, 20 Vauxhall Bridge Road,
London SW1V 2SA

Set in Horley Old Style
by FMT Graphics Limited, Southwark, London
Printed and bound in Singapore
Designed by Polly Dawes
ISBN 0 7126 4595 0

THE JANE HISSEY
COLLECTION

OLD BEAR
ADDRESS BOOK

EBURY PRESS STATIONERY

This book belongs to

Name _____

Address _____

_____

_____

_____

A

Name _____

Address _____

_____

_____

☎ _____

Name _____

Address _____

_____

_____

☎ _____

Name _____

Address _____

_____

_____

☎ _____

Name _____

Address _____

_____

_____

☎ _____

Name _____

Address _____

_____

_____

☎ _____

Name _____

Address _____

_____

_____

☎ _____

Name _____

Address _____

_____

_____

☎ _____

Name _____

Address _____

_____

_____

☎ _____

Name _____

Address _____

_____

_____

☎ _____

Name _____

Address _____

_____

_____

☎ _____

Name _____

Address _____

_____

_____

☎ _____

Name _____

Address _____

_____

_____

☎ _____

B

Name ⸻

Address ⸻

⸻

⸻

☎ ⸻

Name ⸻

Address ⸻

⸻

⸻

☎ ⸻

Name ⸻

Address ⸻

⸻

⸻

☎ ⸻

Name ⸻

Address ⸻

⸻

⸻

☎ ⸻

Name _____

Address _____

_____

_____

☎ _____

Name _____

Address _____

_____

_____

☎ _____

Name _____

Address _____

_____

_____

☎ _____

Name _____

Address _____

_____

_____

☎ _____

Name _____

Address _____

_____

_____

☎ _____

Name _____

Address _____

_____

_____

☎ _____

Name _____

Address _____

_____

_____

☎ _____

Name _____

Address _____

_____

_____

☎ _____

C

Name _____

Address _____

_____

_____

☎ _____

Name _____

Address _____

_____

_____

☎ _____

Name _____

Address _____

_____

_____

☎ _____

Name _____

Address _____

_____

_____

☎ _____

Name _____

Address _____

_____

_____

☎ _____

Name _____

Address _____

_____

_____

☎ _____

Name _____

Address _____

_____

_____

☎ _____

Name _____

Address _____

_____

_____

☎ _____

Name _____

Address _____

_____

_____

☎ _____

Name _____

Address _____

_____

_____

☎ _____ _____

Name _____

Address _____

_____

_____

☎ _____

Name _____

Address _____

_____

_____

☎ _____

D

Name _____

Address _____

_____

_____

☎ _____

Name _____

Address _____

_____

_____

☎ _____

Name _____

Address _____

_____

_____

☎ _____

Name _____

Address _____

_____

_____

☎ _____

Name _____

Address _____

_____

_____

☎ _____

Name _____

Address _____

_____

_____

☎ _____

Name _____

Address _____

_____

_____

☎ _____

Name _____

Address _____

_____

_____

☎ _____

Name _____

Address _____

_____

_____

☎ _____

Name _____

Address _____

_____

_____

☎ _____

Name _____

Address _____

_____

_____

☎ _____

Name _____

Address _____

_____

_____

☎ _____

E

Name _____

Address _____

_____

_____

☎ _____

Name _____

Address _____

_____

_____

☎ _____

Name _____

Address _____

_____

_____

☎ _____

Name _____

Address _____

_____

_____

☎ _____

Name _____

Address _____

_____

_____

☎ _____

Name _____

Address _____

_____

_____

☎ _____

Name _____

Address _____

_____

_____

☎ _____

Name _____

Address _____

_____

_____

☎ _____

Name _____

Address _____

_____

_____

☎ _____

Name _____

Address _____

_____

_____

☎ _____

Name _____

Address _____

_____

_____

☎ _____

Name _____

Address _____

_____

_____

☎ _____

F

Name _____

Address _____

_____

_____

☎ _____

Name _____

Address _____

_____

_____

☎ _____

Name _____

Address _____

_____

_____

☎ _____

Name _____

Address _____

_____

_____

☎ _____

Name _____

Address _____

_____

_____

☎ _____

Name _____

Address _____

_____

_____

☎ _____

Name _____

Address _____

_____

_____

☎ _____

Name _____

Address _____

_____

_____

☎ _____

Name _____

Address _____

_____

_____

☎ _____

Name _____

Address _____

_____

_____

☎ _____

Name _____

Address _____

_____

_____

☎ _____

Name _____

Address _____

_____

_____

☎ _____

G

Name _____

Address _____

_____

_____

☎ _____

Name _____

Address _____

_____

_____

☎ _____

Name _____

Address _____

_____

_____

☎ _____

Name _____

Address _____

_____

_____

☎ _____

Name _____

Address _____

_____

_____

☎ _____

Name _____

Address _____

_____

_____

☎ _____

Name _____

Address _____

_____

_____

☎ _____

Name _____

Address _____

_____

_____

☎ _____

Name _____

Address _____

_____

_____

☎ _____

Name _____

Address _____

_____

_____

☎ _____

Name _____

Address _____

_____

_____

☎ _____

Name _____

Address _____

_____

_____

☎ _____

H

Name _____

Address _____

_____

_____

☎ _____

Name _____

Address _____

_____

_____

☎ _____

Name _____

Address _____

_____

_____

☎ _____

Name _____

Address _____

_____

_____

☎ _____

Name _____

Address _____

_____

_____

☎ _____

Name _____

Address _____

_____

_____

☎ _____

Name _____

Address _____

_____

_____

☎ _____

Name _____

Address _____

_____

_____

☎ _____

Name _____

Address _____

_____

_____

☎ _____

Name _____

Address _____

_____

_____

☎ _____

Name _____

Address _____

_____

_____

☎ _____

Name _____

Address _____

_____

_____

☎ _____

I

Name _____

Address _____

_____

_____

☎ _____

Name _____

Address _____

_____

_____

☎ _____

Name _____

Address _____

_____

_____

☎ _____

Name _____

Address _____

_____

_____

☎ _____

Name _____

Address _____

_____

_____

☎ _____

Name _____

Address _____

_____

_____

☎ _____

Name _____

Address _____

_____

_____

☎ _____

Name _____

Address _____

_____

_____

☎ _____

Name _____

Address _____

_____

_____

☎ _____

Name _____

Address _____

_____

_____

☎ _____

Name _____

Address _____

_____

_____

☎ _____

Name _____

Address _____

_____

_____

☎ _____

Name _____

Address _____

_____

_____

☎ _____

Name _____

Address _____

_____

_____

☎ _____

Name _____

Address _____

_____

_____

☎ _____

Name _____

Address _____

_____

_____

☎ _____

Name _____

Address _____

_____

_____

☎ _____

Name _____

Address _____

_____

_____

☎ _____

Name _____

Address _____

_____

_____

☎ _____

Name _____

Address _____

_____

_____

☎ _____

Name _____

Address _____

_____

_____

☎ _____

Name _____

Address _____

_____

_____

☎ _____

Name _____

Address _____

_____

_____

☎ _____

Name _____

Address _____

_____

_____

☎ _____

K

Name _____

Address _____

_____

_____

☎ _____

Name _____

Address _____

_____

_____

☎ _____

Name _____

Address _____

_____

_____

☎ _____

Name _____

Address _____

_____

_____

☎ _____

Name _____

Address _____

_____

_____

☎ _____

Name _____

Address _____

_____

_____

☎ _____

Name _____

Address _____

_____

_____

☎ _____

Name _____

Address _____

_____

_____

☎ _____

Name _____

Address _____

_____

_____

☎ _____

Name _____

Address _____

_____

_____

☎ _____

Name _____

Address _____

_____

_____

☎ _____

Name _____

Address _____

_____

_____

☎ _____

L

Name _____

Address _____

_____

_____

☎ _____

Name _____

Address _____

_____

_____

☎ _____

Name _____

Address _____

_____

_____

☎ _____

Name _____

Address _____

_____

_____

☎ _____

Name _____

Address _____

_____

_____

☎ _____

Name _____

Address _____

_____

_____

☎ _____

Name _____

Address _____

_____

_____

☎ _____

Name _____

Address _____

_____

_____

☎ _____

Name _____

Address _____

_____

_____

☎ _____

Name _____

Address _____

_____

_____

☎ _____

Name _____

Address _____

_____

_____

☎ _____

Name _____

Address _____

_____

_____

☎ _____

M

Name _____

Address _____

_____

_____

☎ _____

Name _____

Address _____

_____

_____

☎ _____

Name _____

Address _____

_____

_____

☎ _____

Name _____

Address _____

_____

_____

☎ _____

Name _____

Address _____

_____

_____

☎ _____

Name _____

Address _____

_____

_____

☎ _____

Name _____

Address _____

_____

_____

☎ _____

Name _____

Address _____

_____

_____

☎ _____

Name _____

Address _____

_____

_____

☎ _____

Name _____

Address _____

_____

_____

☎ _____

Name _____

Address _____

_____

_____

☎ _____

Name _____

Address _____

_____

_____

☎ _____

N

Name _____

Address _____

_____

_____

☎ _____

Name _____

Address _____

_____

_____

☎ _____

Name _____

Address _____

_____

_____

☎ _____

Name _____

Address _____

_____

_____

☎ _____

Name _____

Address _____

_____

_____

☎ _____

Name _____

Address _____

_____

_____

☎ _____

Name _____

Address _____

_____

_____

☎ _____

Name _____

Address _____

_____

_____

☎ _____

Name _____

Address _____

_____

_____

☎ _____

Name _____

Address _____

_____

_____

☎ _____

Name _____

Address _____

_____

_____

☎ _____

Name _____

Address _____

_____

_____

☎ _____

Name _____

Address _____

_____

_____

☎ _____

Name _____

Address _____

_____

_____

☎ _____

Name _____

Address _____

_____

_____

☎ _____

Name _____

Address _____

_____

_____

☎ _____

Name _____

Address _____

_____

_____

☎ _____

Name _____

Address _____

_____

_____

☎ _____

Name _____

Address _____

_____

_____

☎ _____

Name _____

Address _____

_____

_____

☎ _____

Name _____

Address _____

_____

_____

☎ _____

Name _____

Address _____

_____

_____

☎ _____

Name _____

Address _____

_____

_____

☎ _____

Name _____

Address _____

_____

_____

☎ _____

P

Name _____

Address _____

_____

_____

☎ _____

Name _____

Address _____

_____

_____

☎ _____

Name _____

Address _____

_____

_____

☎ _____

Name _____

Address _____

_____

_____

☎ _____

Name _____

Address _____

_____

_____

☎ _____

Name _____

Address _____

_____

_____

☎ _____

Name _____

Address _____

_____

_____

☎ _____

Name _____

Address _____

_____

_____

☎ _____

Name _____

Address _____

_____

_____

☎ _____

Name _____

Address _____

_____

_____

☎ _____

Name _____

Address _____

_____

_____

☎ _____

Name _____

Address _____

_____

_____

☎ _____

Q

Name _____

Address _____

_____

_____

☎ _____

Name _____

Address _____

_____

_____

☎ _____

Name _____

Address _____

_____

_____

☎ _____

Name _____

Address _____

_____

_____

☎ _____

Name _____

Address _____

_____

_____

☎ _____

Name _____

Address _____

_____

_____

☎ _____

Name _____

Address _____

_____

_____

☎ _____

Name _____

Address _____

_____

_____

☎ _____

Name _____

Address _____

_____

_____

☎ _____

Name _____

Address _____

_____

_____

☎ _____

Name _____

Address _____

_____

_____

☎ _____

Name _____

Address _____

_____

_____

☎ _____

R

Name _____

Address _____

_____

_____

☎ _____

Name _____

Address _____

_____

_____

☎ _____

Name _____

Address _____

_____

_____

☎ _____

Name _____

Address _____

_____

_____

☎ _____

Name _____

Address _____

_____

_____

☎ _____

Name _____

Address _____

_____

_____

☎ _____

Name _____

Address _____

_____

_____

☎ _____

Name _____

Address _____

_____

_____

☎ _____

Name _____

Address _____

_____

_____

☎ _____

Name _____

Address _____

_____

_____

☎ _____

Name _____

Address _____

_____

_____

☎ _____

Name _____

Address _____

_____

_____

☎ _____

S

Name _____

Address _____

_____

_____

☎ _____

Name _____

Address _____

_____

_____

☎ _____

Name _____

Address _____

_____

_____

☎ _____

Name _____

Address _____

_____

_____

☎ _____

Name _____

Address _____

_____

_____

☎ _____

Name _____

Address _____

_____

_____

☎ _____

Name _____

Address _____

_____

_____

☎ _____

Name _____

Address _____

_____

_____

☎ _____

Name _____

Address _____

_____

_____

☎ _____

Name _____

Address _____

_____

_____

☎ _____

Name _____

Address _____

_____

_____

☎ _____

Name _____

Address _____

_____

_____

☎ _____

T

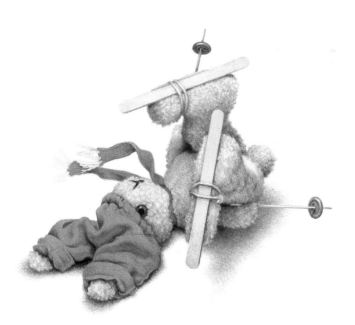

Name _____

Address _____

_____

_____

☎ _____

Name _____

Address _____

_____

_____

☎ _____

Name _____

Address _____

_____

_____

☎ _____

Name _____

Address _____

_____

_____

☎ _____

Name _____

Address _____

_____

_____

☎ _____

Name _____

Address _____

_____

_____

☎ _____

Name _____

Address _____

_____

_____

☎ _____

Name _____

Address _____

_____

_____

☎ _____

Name _____

Address _____

_____

_____

☎ _____

Name _____

Address _____

_____

_____

☎ _____

Name _____

Address _____

_____

_____

☎ _____

Name _____

Address _____

_____

_____

☎ _____

U

Name _____

Address _____

_____

_____

☎ _____

Name _____

Address _____

_____

_____

☎ _____

Name _____

Address _____

_____

_____

☎ _____

Name _____

Address _____

_____

_____

☎ _____

Name _____

Address _____

_____

_____

☎ _____

Name _____

Address _____

_____

_____

☎ _____

Name _____

Address _____

_____

_____

☎ _____

Name _____

Address _____

_____

_____

☎ _____

Name _____

Address _____

_____

_____

☎ _____

Name _____

Address _____

_____

_____

☎ _____

Name _____

Address _____

_____

_____

☎ _____

Name _____

Address _____

_____

_____

☎ _____

V

Name _____

Address _____

_____

_____

☎ _____

Name _____

Address _____

_____

_____

☎ _____

Name _____

Address _____

_____

_____

☎ _____

Name _____

Address _____

_____

_____

☎ _____

Name _____

Address _____

_____

_____

☎ _____

Name _____

Address _____

_____

_____

☎ _____

Name _____

Address _____

_____

_____

☎ _____

Name _____

Address _____

_____

_____

☎ _____

Name _____

Address _____

_____

_____

☎ _____

Name _____

Address _____

_____

_____

☎ _____

Name _____

Address _____

_____

_____

☎ _____

Name _____

Address _____

_____

_____

☎ _____

WX

Name _____

Address _____

_____

_____

☎ _____

Name _____

Address _____

_____

_____

☎ _____

Name _____

Address _____

_____

_____

☎ _____

Name _____

Address _____

_____

_____

☎ _____

Name _____

Address _____

_____

_____

☎ _____

Name _____

Address _____

_____

_____

☎ _____

Name _____

Address _____

_____

_____

☎ _____

Name _____

Address _____

_____

_____

☎ _____

Name _____

Address _____

_____

_____

☎ _____

Name _____

Address _____

_____

_____

☎ _____

Name _____

Address _____

_____

_____

☎ _____

Name _____

Address _____

_____

_____

☎ _____

YZ

Name _____

Address _____

_____

_____

☎ _____

Name _____

Address _____

_____

_____

☎ _____

Name _____

Address _____

_____

_____

☎ _____

Name _____

Address _____

_____

_____

☎ _____

Name _____

Address _____

_____

_____

☎ _____

Name _____

Address _____

_____

_____

☎ _____

Name _____

Address _____

_____

_____

☎ _____

Name _____

Address _____

_____

_____

☎ _____

Name _____

Address _____

_____

_____

☎ _____

Name _____

Address _____

_____

_____

☎ _____

Name _____

Address _____

_____

_____

☎ _____

Name _____

Address _____

_____

_____

☎ _____